Raising A Winner

Raising A Winner

"The Grow & Go® Theory"

Jacqueleen Crittle

MCP

Mill City Press, Inc.
2301 Lucien Way #415
Maitland, FL 32751
407.339.4217
www.millcitypress.net

Cover photo taken by:
Deshaun (Trig) Adams
He Shoots LyfePhotography

Printed in the United States of America

ISBN-13: 978-1-62952-960-8

To the Crittle Family,
my parents Tessa and Joe,
my former MCP families,
and, most importantly, God.
You are the foundation and the source of my inspira-
tion and motivation, along with being the biggest win-
ners of all.

Contents

Biography

J acqueleen Crittle, known to hundreds of Midwestern families as Momma Crittle, is the founder of the Midwest College Project career and college planning organization and MCP College Connection Dorm Movers, along with being a parenting and college planning advocate extraordinaire.

For more than a decade, Momma Crittle has successfully supported and offered student and parenting resources to over one thousand families within the Midwest. Her wealth of knowledge spans the spectrum from child birth education, Suzuki music instruction, and academic enrichment services to career and college planning, corporate mentoring, and diversity and inclusion matters.

Through partnering efforts with Midwestern universities such as the University of Missouri (Mizzou), Michigan State, the University of Iowa, St. Louis University (SLU), the University of Louisville, and the University of Kentucky, she has been able to forge sustainable relations and rapport to support sending over three hundred students to college.

With multiple post-secondary education degrees and certifications in communications, marketing, health law, nonprofit philanthropic management, and Lean Six Sigma classifications, she has networked to provide both students and families the support that they need.

To learn more about her Midwestern resources, to solicit her support for a public speaking opportunity at a high school or college planning event, visit her website at www.raisingawinner.com or www.themwcp.com

Foreword

The opportunity to write a foreword for my mother is something I would have never imagined. I knew she always wanted to write a book, but I never thought I would be a contributor as well. It makes it special for me to write this because of what the entire book is about—parenting. Parenting is something I have yet to experience, but I know it must be something that only the biggest shoes can fill. Even though I may not understand everything my parents are teaching me, in the long run, their advice always eventually makes sense.

The advice I receive from my parents now at eighteen is basically the same as when I was in preschool. Outside of the rules they set for my sister and me, they each live by three simple mantras: don't bite the hand that feeds you; Grow and Go; and always keep a circle of five.

The saying "don't bite the hand that feeds you" stems from showing gratitude to someone who has contributed to your growth and success. I've learned that piece of advice not only applies to your parents, but to outsiders as well. Anyone that has "fed" you knowledge, material, experience, and opportunity deserves appreciation. Both of my parents always tell me that I never know who I may need in the future, that's why it's so important to express your appreciation to them while you can.

"Grow and Go" is a saying that my mother uses almost daily. She uses it as her mantra for parenting. It basically means that a parent's job is to raise their children and allow them to grow up and experience the realities of life. However, in certain scenarios, growing and going is self-taught. Sometimes it's not the parent who instills life's realities in their child, but the child that experiences life for what it's worth through their own eyes. Although it sounds harsh, it's a part of moving on. If a child decides not to listen to the authoritative figure in their life, they must accept the fact they will have to learn the hard way.

All of these mantras have been used throughout my life, but I believe the advice of keeping a circle of five has resonated with me the most. Keeping a circle of five means to surround yourself with at least five friends or associates that are as smart as—or smarter than—you. They should uplift you, motivate you, and have your best interests at heart. In grammar school, nearly all of my friends were advanced in their extracurricular activities and academics, and that motivated me to stay on top of my work as well, but as I started to grow older,

I made more friends (some of whom were not on my level academically). However, I remember my mom telling me that my circle of five did not always have to be people that were book smart. Even though they may not be book smart, they may have something else to offer. That advice has stayed with me.

The purpose of my applying these mantras is to not only show that my parents were correct, but to prove that raising a winner does not always mean raising someone who is academically advanced. A winner is someone who has integrity, shows humility and compassion, overcomes adversity, has the ability to be their true selves, and so much more. Not even the most intelligent of people demonstrate all of these traits. My parents have hopes and aspirations for my sister and me, but the moment they look at what we have become and not what they wanted us to be is the moment we become winners.

Kayla Marie Crittle

Prologue

Raising a child can be tough. It actually takes *more* than a village to succeed in raising what we like to call a winner. I think it's the unspoken rule of parenting that we all start out attempting to raise a winner. I think it's every parent's hidden desire. However, we must ask ourselves what a winner truly is. Once we know the answer, we can then best identify what we can do as parents to support our children's needs.

I could think of a million ways to describe what I would call a winner, but ultimately, winning is not about what society defines for us; it's about what we define for ourselves. Actually, not so surprisingly, being a winner has nothing to do with the amount of money we earn, the colleges we attended, the degrees we possess, or even the job titles we hold. We know that we are winning once we no longer have fear about our future but can look in the mirror and be happy with the finished product. If we can reflect back on our lives and be proud of the actions that we have taken and the advice we followed to allow us to stand as independent, self-sufficient, productive contributors to society, we are all winners.

Sound good? Well, it should; however, it's not always that simple. For many, including myself, this process is a road with many hurdles that we must travel to arrive at our final destination. They tell me that there isn't any road map to success, but I beg to differ. What I have learned through the years of watching my elders, academic educators, my own parents, family, friends, and even people that I witness or interact with on a daily basis is that the road map lies somewhere in a place that has yet to be documented with pen and paper. It remains in the back of someone's mind, waiting to be shared with you. Today, you are witnessing the fruits of years of working with families with children, during which I have been mentally documenting various short stories — in their words and my own — that will hopefully help a parent, or more importantly, a young person, to be able to Grow and Go.

For the last five years I have selfishly dedicated myself to working with college and career planning for high school students. I say "selfishly" because I have always embraced programming and entrepreneurial business ventures that were in alignment with where my own children were in life. I figured out back in 2003 that if I wanted something for my children that was not readily available, I could simply create it. And, for a time, it appeared to work. My first attempt at fulfilling this void was with an academic and fine arts program based in the suburbs of our community, as I could not find access to the same level of resources that seemed to be readily available some twenty-two miles away in the inner city. I could not bring myself to understand why children in the suburbs would not want access to things such as Suzuki violin, piano, thespian drama, urban dance, or academic enrichment. It seemed to me that the cultural disparity of program offerings from one community to the next was glaringly different. So, I decided to help bridge the gap. For a period of five years I successfully ran an after-school and summer enrichment program that would service some 250 families and three satellite grade school programs. It was during these first five years that I began to witness the variety of parenting styles that may be reminiscent of some of your own experiences. I had embarked upon a journey that my own family would later pay the price for. For the sake of privacy and confidentiality, I share some of these experiences anonymously, or in the words of my interviewees, in order to help you raise or become a winner who will Grow and Go.

As parents, we should not allow our life plan to dictate the choices that our children will make; we have to provide them with the opportunity to make some choices on their own, even when we believe they are too young to make them. We also never want to judge the book by its cover, because a hidden gem could be underneath waiting to be exposed. Again, the goal here is to allow that son or daughter to Grow and Go and make their own friendships, remembering that if we have done our jobs successfully as parents, the foundation we have provided them with will carry over into their decision-making process.

Chapter One

Comfort Buddy

It was one of my first days on the job when a new mom walked into my office to inquire about the program. She wanted to learn a little bit about me and determine what value she thought I might bring to her child's summer experience. Without my asking, she began to share both her and her husband's professional and Ivy League credentials, along with the various boards that they held positions on. She wanted to let me know that they were well-educated and financially successful parents. She went on to tell me that she had hopes of her son becoming a professional musician, as well as an attorney, and that they had a baby grand piano at home. She said that her child was reading several grade levels above his peers and that he was very well rounded, and she was hoping that this program could somehow continue to enrich his learning experience.

I thought for a minute, and I decided to choose my words wisely. I really wanted to say, "He sounds amazing at age six, and so do you! I was wondering if I could hire you to support our programming. You really represent everything that we hope to achieve." After all, I was in charge of a fun and creative atmosphere in which we would accept children of all socioeconomic backgrounds and cultural experiences, and, ideally, many of them would be at varying levels of academic performance. Some students would have parents who were judges, doctors, and lawyers, whereas others would have parents who were bus drivers, administrative assistants, or even stay-at-home moms. Some would come into the program with outstanding talents and capabilities while others would be just beginning to test the waters and tap into their passions. And it was this combined set of experiences that I hoped would make my program participants well rounded.

But I decided to leave all that I out. I simply pulled out a program brochure and began to walk her through the various program offerings and the credentials of all the program instructors and administrators. For whatever reason, it seemed to resonate with her in a way that led her to immediately sign her son up, and even refer a friend or two. I was delighted at the thought of a new client and the dollars that were rolling in—what a great adventure I had tapped into. The most rewarding part was that my own two daughters were able to participate and reap the rewards of such programming right in their own suburban backyard.

Several weeks later I hosted a parent meet and greet, which became my biggest eye opener ever. It was on this day that I learned just how passionate mothers can be about their personal involvement and expectations for their children. It was during this session that I met some wonderful mothers who would become my confidants, my go-to source for guidance and inspiration for supporting the program participants as well as my own children.

On the first day of programming this same mom came to drop off her son, the son was smiling, seemed eager to come inside, and immediately released his mom's hand once he was greeted at the door. The mom, however, proceeded to tell our program director that her son was a bit shy, and she was wondering if she might sit in on the first few minutes of the day so that he would begin to feel comfortable. My program director at the time was a forty-year veteran in the academic sector and gave me an "Are you kidding me?" look, but again, in my desire to keep her support of the program, I allowed her to come inside. I watched from a distant glass door as she asked her son where he would like to sit, and she made her way toward another young man who was even happier than her son. The two young men met each other with a smile as the mom made eye contact with another little boy whose parents she knew; she had referred him to the program. Immediately, she jerked her son away and asked him to sit next to the familiar friend. All I could do was shake my head. I can recall asking myself, "Why not cut your losses now and just give her money back?" Had I done the right thing by allowing her to come inside? What started out as a five- to ten-minute request had turned into the first thirty minutes of the day.

Finally, after making eye contact with the administrator, who looked at the clock and then back at me, I knew I needed to make a move. I stepped inside, called the mom by name, and asked her to come to my office. I watched as she looked at her son and told him, "You two stick together," and walked away. As she entered my office, I assured her that everything seemed to be going well and that it appeared that her son had indeed linked up with a "comfort buddy" and should be fine. She agreed and left my office to carry out her day.

Later on, I found myself back in the music room as the children were beginning group exposure to either piano or violin. I immediately drew my attention to the young man from the morning, discovering that he was no longer with his comfort buddy but had made his way back to his smiling friend from the morning. The two of them seemed to have become fast friends, asking to eat lunch together and joining in on most activities as a tag team. I looked around for the friend that the mom had chosen and noticed that he was running around in circles and the counselors were struggling to get him to settle down. Once they did get him to settle down, he didn't seem to be interested in much. My goal would be to keep a watchful eye on him in the coming days and try to identify things that he might have interest in. I had never had a son, but I knew that some boys could be pretty rambunctious, so I would pray for patience and that my staff didn't quit before the end of summer.

In the meantime, it was pickup time, and, as to be expected, our mom was back—twenty minutes before the regular dismissal. I can't say that I was the least bit surprised. She again came inside and shared that she came early to see how things were going. I told her that to avoid disrupting the group she might observe from a distance behind the glass door. To her surprise, her son was not with the family friend but was with a new comfort buddy. She swiftly moved into my office and asked me how all the children were grouped. I pointed out that we first look at age, then special interest, and later, once the academic component begins, they would be assessed and aligned with similar performers. I will never forget my emotions when she said, "Then I'm not quite sure how my son is not with the Bradley boy, as both their parents listen to classical music, we belong to the same country club, we even attended graduate school together, and at home our boys play together quite often. I'm certain they would have very similar interests." Many thoughts ran through my mind at this moment. The first was, "Lord, give me strength not to let this woman have it." After all, it had been a long day, and the Bradley boy had succeeded in working the nerves of every single employee I had hired that summer, including me. Furthermore, I could not believe that a parent would have so little regard for understanding that who parents associate with and what special interests they might share would have absolutely no bearing on the acquaintances or interests a child would develop on their own. What I said next shocked even me.

I told her, "You're right. That sometimes is the case. We shall see how things progress tomorrow." I chose to pick my battles and lived to be open for another day of business. Once she left my office, I could not believe that I was supporting this idiotic way of thinking. I could not believe that anyone would have this type of thought process. So, later that day, I met with my advisory team and I shared my experience. It was during this session that our team psychologist shared that I should handle this in a diplomatic method that would allow the parent to visually experience the young man's choices without saying a word. With much resistance from the staff, we decided to try this approach.

That evening I called the parent in question and said, "We would like to offer you the opportunity to sit as an observer for any portion of the day that you like. However, you would not be allowed in the room, only to observe behind the scenes." Not so surprisingly, she was delighted and agreed. The next day, shortly before lunch, she arrived and took her position in an incon-spicuous spot that would not allow her son to witness her presence, but allowed her a direct view of him. She watched as the Bradley boy went from table to table, seemingly annoying most of his peers, while her own child took his position to eat next to his comfort buddy. At that moment, our music teacher arrived early with a music case in hand that appeared to be a flute or clarinet of some sort. The instructor asked if he might join the lunch session, and of course I agreed. The mom and I sat and anxiously watched what he was doing with this instrument case, because we only offered violin and piano. Would we be in for a treat? To our surprise, he handed the instrument to the comfort buddy. The com-fort buddy took the flute out of the case, stepped center stage, and began to play. Was this Little Stevie Wonder or what? We were both completely blown away; com-fort buddy was no more than seven years old, and he was playing like a concert musician. The whole roomed clapped in amazement. I could see the awe in the mom's eyes as she witnessed the same musical genius.

Sometime later, the Bradley boy made his way to his family friend, and they talked for a while but soon went their separate ways. Finally, the mom had seen enough; she said she needed to return to work and thanked me for the invitation. The next day, her son was dropped off at the door with no mom in sight. He exited the car and she hugged him goodbye and pulled out. I was certain she had to go to the bathroom and simply could not wait any longer. To my surprise, once inside the son handed me a small envelope and went about his way. I slowly opened the note as I walked back into my office. I will simply share this: "I had no idea how similar but different our sons' interests were. My son told me all about his new friend last night and it turns out I've encountered his mom on occasion as she works at a local department store I frequent. Now I have a play date to plan. Keep up the good work!" I could not believe what I was reading. The tables had turned, and I hadn't said a word. I was sure that this would be the first of many eye openers for this mother, as she had several other children at home, but it was a welcomed epiphany.

That summer would go on and I would soon learn many more life and parenting lessons, but this was a lesson that would stay with me for life. I would learn not to judge by what I wanted for my children, but by what they wanted for themselves. I must say that this lesson is still one that is actively in play; I've watched my daughters make both good and bad decisions over the years, but I always reflect back on the comfort buddy and his family to teach me not to judge the book by its cover.

Some of the best parenting is done by mother figures; however, sometimes the best parenting can happen through the actions of a father. The harsh truth is that in today's society, many fathers are forced to act as mother figures and rear their children, and their journey is often a story that goes untold. A real father who stands up and takes his place as the sole provider and nurturer for his children is the most commendable, and we don't see it often enough.

The names of the families have been changed to protect the identity of everyone involved in the next chapter, but the story is very real. So, don't let the title fool you; female parents, grandparents, or siblings most often represent mother figures in our culture. Moms can also come in the form of a male parent who is acting in the absence of a mother. I had the opportunity to experience this along my journey more than once. However, one family really left a lasting impression upon me and best represents a true depiction of the Grow and Go theory.

Chapter Two

Mr. Mom

Several years ago, I made the acquaintance of a father who had been raising his daughter alone since her birth. It was odd, because the mother was still alive and well, but she felt so bitter toward the father that she decided to give up her parental rights and simply allow the dad to do his thing while she quietly remained in the background with minimal or no involvement. I would often ask myself how a mother could take such actions, but I knew from witnessing so many families with broken homes that you can never really judge from the outside looking in. You can never know that person's story; therefore, I refrained from judgment. Because I know there are always two sides to every story, I won't focus on the level of engagement shown by the mother, but more on the father's desire to raise a winner.

At our first encounter, I could tell that this father was super serious about the details of life and his passion to raise a poised, intellectual, and well-rounded young woman. From first glance, it appeared that he had done an outstanding job. Starting at a very early age for his daughter, he was the "mom" who couldn't comfortably ask other young girls to spend the night or join the mothers' committee for school-based activities, because it would be deemed inappropriate. He maintained his position with the cards both he and his daughter had been dealt. In fact, his daughter had not been exposed to a lot of things that other young girls may have experienced with their female peers. Things like sleepovers, play dates, and the chatter of girls' gossip were simply not a part of their world.

As fate would have it, Mr. Mom became immersed in all things Amy. The chores in the home were equally divided between the two of them, and it was expected that both parties carry them out with precision and attention to detail so that Amy would learn to properly manage a home and care for herself. His military background had most certainly carried over into his parenting style. I could see from the very beginning that Amy was miserable; her forced hermit-like behavior had given her a permanent scowl. It became rare to see Amy smile, and she was always reluctant to take photographs, although she was very photogenic.

Meanwhile, Mr. Mom had avoided publicly dating for many years to spare Amy from witnessing the highs and lows of his romantic relationships. Amy was indeed not a fan of his dating and was critical of every partner she somehow got wind of. As a result, dating as a whole was not a topic of discussion which Amy felt comfortable having with a father. As time went on, the awkwardness around the dating discussion became even more of an issue, as Dad could tell that his daughter was indeed becoming a beautiful young woman whom any young man would find attractive.

Amy did like many young girls her age and kept many secrets about her emotions, only finding solace with a few select friends who she felt she could share her thoughts with from time to time. But even with her female friends, she remained guarded. She never shared her true feelings with anyone, either acting in secrecy or avoiding the discussion altogether, which led to difficulty making female friends. Mr. Mom's fatherly instincts went into overdrive, and he broadcast that no one was good enough for his Amy. He set boundaries and expectations so high that some might say they were unrealistic—or just plain insane. He wanted to meet everyone that his daughter might even have a brief conversation with. When he saw he was getting nowhere with Amy, he decided to breach the unspoken boundary and become involved with extracurricular activities where, traditionally, only female moms had been involved.

What was he thinking? Mr. Mom was everywhere that his daughter didn't want him to be. The kids at school thought he was super cool, but Amy said she saw him as a super fool. Special moments in time, such as school dances and prom, became less interesting to Amy because she didn't want to deal with Mr. Mom's scrutiny or involvement. I often found her actions to be odd, but I never challenged them, because at that age anything is conceivable. All young girls can be hormonal and obstinate. I worried that Amy was passing up opportunities that she would never have the chance to "do over." But Amy had made up her mind; despite her dad's encouragement to attend these events, she remained cold and stubborn. Her answer was still "no." As a result, she never attended any dances or prom.

When it came time for high school graduation, Amy was excited about the possibility of exploring a career in marketing. Amy had been involved in many marketing projects over the years and had become quite gifted in the arena, earning tremendous awards and accolades. When the college application process began, Amy had researched all of the top marketing programs in the country. Most were far away from home — except one. Amy was ready to spread her wings. However, her dad had his own ideas.

Mr. Mom had become consumed by the idea of her attending an Ivy League institution. Now don't get me wrong: Amy was a decent student, but probably not high-pressure Ivy League material. It was clear that Mr. Mom had his own ideas about Amy's future, and he wasn't about to let up. The battle between father and daughter went on for months until Amy, with much dismay, chose a school on the West Coast, passing up her admission to one of the top marketing schools in the country. Amy was disappointed in her decision, but shared that she was accepting of it as well, because she would have the chance to go away.

After graduation, I wondered about the longevity of the precious father-daughter relationship that had been forged over the years. I recently heard from Amy and learned that during the first full semester of college she avoided full contact with Mr. Mom, so that she could make decisions without his scrutiny, judgment, and hovering. It was disappointing to hear, as we all know how important that first year away can be, not only for the student but for the family. I can recall cleaving to the phone, waiting to hear the exciting stories and new developments from my own college student, so I can't even imagine how disappointing it must have been for Mr. Mom.

With all these emotions, I understood Amy's deep-seated desire to find herself and be able to spread her wings. Over the years, she had unconsciously become the "wife" to her dad, who was so set on putting every-thing he had into raising his child that he often forgot about giving time to himself, as well as time for her to make decisions for herself. I've learned so much from this particular family. It's so important to allow our children to make some choices on their own and even allow for some bumps in the road because it's *their* life. We also have to give ourselves space to be ourselves so we don't become consumed with our children's lives to the point that we cease having a life of our own.

In the end, Amy missed her dad deeply, and she never ceased loving him, but Amy had finally found the opportunity to allow herself to Grow and Go. Recently, Amy transferred to a new school and is still somewhat distant from her father. As for Mr. Mom, I recently spoke to him and he shared that, although he was disappointed by the lack of communication, it had actually given him time to self-evaluate and recapture his own life. He finally began to date, travel, and do the things that he had been missing over the years that he had raised Amy. He told me he would not trade being Mr. Mom for the world; it was a once in a lifetime opportunity to mold, share, and raise a child, but he was now grateful for the time to get to know himself. Sometimes, we give so much that we forget to give to ourselves. I am grateful to see Amy successfully Grow and Go.

Often, we are called to trust our instincts. We have to learn to trust that the role models that we have served as are enough to give our children what they need as sponges to develop into well-rounded, kindhearted adults. It's awesome when two parents are present to raise a child, but in today's society it's not always an option. It's important to be aware that our children are watching our every move, learning about the adult they choose to become, learning how to treat people, and learning how to navigate life. We as parents should feel confident that when we make the right moves in life while our children are watching, they will one day emulate this behavior. This next journey is a true personal account that warms my heart. A mother's life lesson is made clear from the words and actions of her very own son.

Chapter Three

Am I My Mother's Keeper?

Merina had worked her whole life without much help from any outsiders, and she was proud of all her life's accomplishments. She had successfully taken herself outside of the South Side housing projects where she had been raised and was determined to provide a better life for herself. Hard work and dedication had proven to serve her well. She had her own private practice and a PhD in psychology, and she was working hard to remain successful. Three years into running her private practice, she met a guy who seemed to be perfect in all aspects: he was charming, well dressed, and drove a new Mercedes C Class. He had a very solid, well-paying career, and he owned his home. He was what most women would be looking for in terms of dating.

Merina was, like most mothers, reluctant to introduce her new male suitor to her son. Dating in the past had not gone very well. She had avoided providing him with exposure to other men since his own father had passed away many years prior. She worried that bringing new men into her life might lead to competition or jealousy. She was always unsure if any man would be suitable as a stepfather or mentor for her son, so she simply avoided contact. But this time would be different. Merina called and consulted our sisterhood of friends about the worthiness of her new male companion, and I must admit she appeared to have met Mr. Right. I can hear myself saying, "Hey, the verdict's not out on this guy," and I was always the pessimist in my friend group. So, we all agreed to give him a month or two to see how things would progress and then, if everything was still tracking, it would be fine to introduce him to Merina's son. As fate would have it, things worked out and the two met.

It wasn't too long before things took a turn for the worse. Her son, whom I'll refer to as Walter, wasn't performing well in school. He had always been a good student before. Maybe it was the switch to a new high school. Whatever the reason, his performance in school had quickly declined. Merina found herself in the new and awkward position of trying to discipline a son who had never received so much as a slap or punishment. The arguments began to occur almost daily. I could see my friend unraveling, so one of our mutual friends suggested that she have her new guy talk to Walter man-to-man to determine what the root cause might be for this abrupt change in behavior. The new guy seemed delighted to jump in and offer support. So Merina set up a family luncheon one Saturday, and her new guy offered up tickets to a Cubs game for himself and Walter. Walter immediately said no, he wasn't interested. Merina thought his response was disrespectful and rude, so she forced Walter to attend.

During their time together, Merina's new male friend discovered that Walter was rebelling because he didn't want the new guy in the picture. It had been ten years of just Walter and Merina, and he simply wanted it to stay that way. Walter told him that he really didn't want his mother dating anyone and that no one could ever replace his dad. I'm guessing they watched the rest of the game in silence.

When they returned home, Merina had been waiting. She knew things had not gone well when Walter walked into the house without a word and headed straight to his room. I had been there the whole evening, consoling my friend, and I could not believe my eyes. The young man that I affectionately called "nephew" had become someone I hardly knew. As Merina approached her guy, he shook his head and said that maybe it wasn't the right time for them to continue dating, maybe he needed some space and time. I can never forget the look on Merina's face as her eyes welled up and she mouthed to me, "What's happening here?"

As soon as her guy left, I knew I had to do something.

I went to Walter's room and said, "So, I hear you are not a fan of your mother's new boyfriend."

He said, "Isn't it obvious?"

When I asked why, he said that he was dating someone else.

I said, "Who's dating someone else?"

"Who do you think?"

"Walter, that's a pretty cheap shot. Why would you say such a thing and ruin your mother's happiness?"

What he said next really pulled at my heartstrings. He shared that all his life he had wanted a father figure, someone that he could confide in and learn about dating from and play sports with. Most importantly, he wanted someone to make his mother smile. He said that with all the "things" they had, his mother never really seemed happy; she seemed like some part of her died with his dad and that she put herself into her work simply to avoid feeling lonely. Walter shared that his mom used him as the excuse for why she would not date when the truth was that she was afraid for herself. I could see the hurt and anguish in his face when I asked, "But how do you know that this guy is not the right one and, more importantly, how would you know he's dating someone else?"

"He's my classmate's stepfather," said Walter.

My immediate response was, "You waited until *now* to share this?"

Apparently, his suspicions arose two weeks earlier when he saw his classmate dropped off at school in a familiar car, but the driver took off so fast that he couldn't get a good look. Walter had started going in extra early every day since then to try and catch a glimpse of the man behind the wheel. A few days earlier, his suspicions were confirmed. He asked his friend who the man who dropped her off was, and she said it was her stepdad. He told her he had not seen him before, and she informed him that her mom had been away for work for several weeks and he was now doing drop-off.

I struggled with the best way to tell my friend. I realized that the burden Walter had been carrying needed to be lifted. I told him to plan some time once we left to sit down and share these findings with his mom. He was now in tears, fearful of the disappointment and hurt that he would be responsible for bringing to his mother. He had experienced many sleepless nights that were causing him to lose focus in class, and, in turn, were impacting his grades.

A few days later, I got a phone call from my friend. I had been expecting it. I could tell she was choosing her words wisely as she began to tell me the details of the story I already knew. Merina told me that Walter had made her proud, and he had given her the courage to be honest with herself. She told me that she had some suspicions, but cast them aside because she was finally happy. Even without a man around as a role model, Walter had developed the traits of a real man, complete with honor, dignity, respect, honesty, and compassion for women.

Merina said, "I worried for years no man would be a good enough role model and replacement for Walter's father, but I've learned that good parenting can come from observation and innate good character. My son had become a man, while I had my eyes closed on the sidelines as a mother."

In life, there are no certainties. We plan ahead for our children, however, we never think about planning for a life without one another. At times, we move through life as if tomorrow is promised to us. It's sad when it's not!

This next short tells of a father's journey to raise his children alone with faith, encouragement, and the sometimes unsolicited support from family. I'm certain that his spouse is looking down on him for a job well done. If you are a single parent and you feel like all hope is gone when raising your children, take a page from his life to help you move through your own.

Chapter Four

No Contingency Plan—It's God's Plan

Over the years you meet some families that really make an impression on you. They become like family and you embrace them in a way that you would your own. Back in 2008, I met a male coworker who made such an impression. Really, it was more his wife that I took a liking to— maybe because we had gone to the same college, maybe because we belonged to the same sorority, or maybe because we had children almost the exact same age. You name it, I could think of so many similarities that would draw us toward one another as friends. But I think what drew me in the most was her love for the Lord and her kind, loving personality.

I knew from the very beginning that my friend was not well. After all, she had divulged to our sisterhood of friends the story of how she lost her own mom as a child due to heart failure and had sadly inherited the very same health condition. But this was a new era, and medicine had made so many advances that I could not even begin to think about the unthinkable. As fate would have it, her husband, who was a good buddy of mine, once shared that he never had a contingency plan either. He never prepared for the death of a spouse. In fact, with the death of his wife, his home became a contingency plan for his parents, more of a second home for them. His parents lost sight of the individual family he created; they felt like it was their family to make decisions for. His own mom was manipulating him in a way to hold hostage her affection to get him to do what she wanted him to do. My friend did not plan for this to happen. I can recall that it was something as simple as a visit to the doctor to attain shots to enroll in junior high that would quickly open my friend's eyes. He would say to me, "The thing about being a mother is that women do the little things that men aren't pro-grammed to do." He was lost and heartbroken, and it became difficult to witness.

I can recall on one such occasion when he shared that he was built to be married, and his one true love was now gone. He somehow felt empty without a spouse by his side. It was this feeling that made it so challenging as he set out to find companionship for himself. After all, being a single parent was a shock. So, he prayed on it. My friend would tell me that he had his church home, and they were not as opinionated as the people closer to him, such as his wife's friends or his own family. The church was more understanding, but even with their understanding it was still the big talk of the church when he began to date just eight months after her death.

Just sitting down and thinking about everything, he told his sons, Derrick and James: "I need you to mature faster than your peers." "I need you to be more independent by helping yourselves." "I can't be both your mom and your dad."

None of this seemed to help, because these were still young boys who were saddened by the loss of their mom, and they were still at the age where they were destined to be knuckleheaded. But with each passing day he became stronger as a father. He found that he was not the same person; he matured after his wife passed. He had to act and go beyond what he wanted for himself. I never questioned what happened next, because I knew that her praying spirit was still very much a part of his daily life. The prayers became almost daily out of the fear and worry about what he should do. Then it happened—the best advice that was ever given to him came from an unlikely source. A friend asked, "Did your wife ever work? If so, go to the Social Security office and file for her social security benefits." He did, and it was there he found out that each child was entitled to $900 per month without taxes. This helped in ways he could not imagine; he shared with me that he could feel his wife looking down to give him a hand. And just as she had frugally managed their household budget, he would continue to be mindful of his spending. In the back of his mind, he always knew that the Social Security payments would end at some point, so he tried to save for the future. However, money would not give him all the answers. He wished there was some kind of book that could tell him what to do next. Looking back on things, it was clear James and Derrick were still missing their mom. They were grieving in their own way. My friend had gotten his boys some counseling and was told during those sessions not to press them, because there would be times they'd appreciate being quiet and times they would not want to talk about anything. As time went on, this too became a challenge, because my friend felt in the dark on many matters of their heart.

My friend could have a temper, and I think it was one of the hardest aspects of their father-son relationships to deal with. There was a tall task ahead of them. He would constantly tell the boys, "I am not mom. I am Dad, and not your maid." Female friends would advise him to set up chores and nice allowances with consequences; otherwise, things weren't going to change. I would laugh when he would call me and say, "These boys are nasty as hell." Once he told me that he remembered going into his sons' bathroom after a year and thinking, "Did a baby whale bathe in oil in this tub?" It was just insanity. But being a mother with daughters, I would tell him, "Praise God that it's two boys, because you wouldn't know where or how to manage with two girls." But life has a funny way of lining things up and preparing us for our futures. When my buddy's wife was in and out of the hospital, we know now that he was being prepared or trained to make meals, help with homework, deal with day-to-day family issues, and become the replacement mother.

Yet, with all the support, guidance, and even the slight preparation, if there was an area that he could have done better with it was those moments when his sons needed a woman's touch. "Women are like water, and men are like iron," he would say. James and Derrick were missing the water, hence the importance of two parents in the household.

He was hard on them a lot, and his actions weren't necessarily the right approach. He learned that his lack of acceptance, high expectations, and not saying "I love you" were huge missteps. It was challenging, but he once again leaned on the church for guidance to support his ability to say, "I'm here for you. Even when your eyes are rolling and you are mad at the world, I'm here." He read somewhere that statistics show that male children who received a hug and a kiss on the cheek turned out more well-rounded and compassionate, which prompted him to do it more often. It's funny, but the boys would see this action as their father being

Mr. Goofy Dad, but somehow it became the method to his madness.

Trying to be a role model was not an easy thing to do, but I watched as his boys did the right things, and he really tried to be more accepting and praising. Recently, Derrick brought home a girl he was dating from college. He drove from New Orleans to St. Louis with her family. It wasn't just an interaction; we could tell the girl's family knew his son. I could tell he felt like an outsider. Two weeks later, when they were home for summer break, they broke up. As a father, he tried to comfort his son, but he was frustrated. He attempted to give advice, like "Gauge your priorities." I can remember him telling them, "School is your first priority, and you're using part of my credit score to be at college." What a laughable moment! Who is thinking about credit when your heart is broken at that age? But it was all he could give, and somehow, his sons accepted it.

Many years have passed since I lost my friend, their mother and his wife, and I have watched as he prepared to send them to prom, then graduation, and now college. I was not surprised when both boys chose her alma mater. Many people never expected either son to go to the same school, but I did. I knew what others didn't, and that was that each boy had a yearning to bond with their mother once again. James planned to attend UC

Davis like his dad, but it had become very competitive, especially with other in-state applicants. When the news finally came of his denial, it was somewhat of a relief. With the denial letter in hand, he became more focused on his new journey at Xavier University. This was really no surprise, because everyone knew he liked Xavier, and it was a natural fit, especially since his brother was there as well.

The boys have been true to their masculinity. They've done things such as; sneaking girls in the basement overnight and dating multiple girls at one time. They have had their share of hiccups, but their dad asked family and friends to help coach and talk to them about how to be careful, or avoiding becoming teen parents. His philosophy was, "Get into a relationship with God. Not a relationship with religion, but with God. It's about sacrifice and spending time getting to know God and staying in touch with God." This family had a praying wife and mother, and that aspect has remained true. In fact, it has been the constant in how these sons have been raised. My friend always told me, "My sons have no choice while under my roof, but through my leadership, I'm going to try to show them the best way."

This year, as they both headed off to college, I saw two strong, handsome, God-fearing young men who respect women and society and have a mindset to reach for the stars. And I think about the fact that they may not have been equipped with a contingency plan, but they were certainly well prepared with God's plan to go out and Grow and Go.

The life of the single mother is often filled with strength, courage, and triumph. A mother successfully raising three sons in today's society is nothing short of a miracle. The crime, violence, and negative outside influences are every mother's greatest fear. Every once in a great while we find those mothers who are facing these tragedies head on by raising boys into men. These life lessons are even sweeter when these young men break down the cultural barriers, overcome the greatest adversity, and win at life. The next chapter tells a compelling heartfelt story in the participants own voice.

Chapter Five

You Never Gave Up on Me

I am a single divorced mother and have been for thirteen years. I have three sons and an adopted son from a current relationship. I divorced in 2004. I decided to leave my then-spouse due to an affair that led to him fathering another child, who is the same age as my oldest son. It was a very bitter, nasty divorce. Our relationship could not go forward once he was found to be the father.

Ultimately, I have been forced to raise my children as a single mother in my hometown of Chicago. Leaving a home that I knew and trusted with only $8000 in my pocket, I put my own education on the back burner to help save money, and I sacrificed to provide a better life for my children. I started college in Ohio, but I was never able to finish what I started.

In 2004 I began my new life with my three sons. My move to Chicago was to one of the poorest communities in the nation, and I struggled to make a way for my sons. The environment victimized my oldest son. My children were twelve, nine, and four years of age at this time. They were innocent suburban children who had been growing up in an upper middle income environment in Cleveland, Ohio, so this was a huge shift for them.

The boys were enrolled in school and life was good for the first six months. In the fall of 2004, I enrolled in college at Chicago State University. The boys started to have relationship issues with their father based upon the distance, which caused them to wonder if this move to Chicago was a good move. Birthdays and Christmas came around with no dad; he really dropped the ball with the father-son relationships. As a result, I stepped up to the plate to be both mom and dad. Every single Sunday, going to church with the entire family became my ritualistic routine.

It was rough, so I decided to move six months later. I felt that the environment really impacted how the boys saw themselves and what they expected for their future, because a lot of their friends in Chicago Heights, where we lived, really weren't going anywhere. One of them actually committed suicide in his home in front of his family.

So we moved to Park Forest, Illinois, thinking that this would bring a new life. The boys were active in school and community activities such as baseball, basketball, and football. Life was back to normal. Everyone had their own room in our new townhome.

Not even a week after living there, my oldest son ran away. Life didn't change for my oldest—he had been captured by the environment of Chicago Heights. I walked the streets at night with a bat five or six times, just looking for my son. Finally, after so many run-away attempts, I decided to report the last one to the police. They, in turn, turned the case over to the juvenile system. My son was now in the system as a juvenile runaway. I signed him up for school counseling and as an ADHD child with an IEP plan, but he would leave school or avoid attendance. His self-esteem dropped, his attendance was worse, and he got involved with a gang. The initiation involved him stealing things to take back to the gang leader. However, he was never able to join the gang because his truancy in school caught up with him. He was caught and assigned to the juvenile detention center in Joliet, Illinois. He spent some time there as a fourteen-year-old.

It was 2006, my oldest was fourteen, soon to turn fifteen, and he was already a runaway in the system. At this point he had not been caught for stealing, but for sleeping in cars and abandoned homes. So, once he spent his first stint in the juvenile system he got a wake-up call. I told him I would only visit him once. But two years later, it was still the same thing. He was sixteen, and he'd finally been caught stealing. Now he'd been charged with a juvenile felony from stealing in someone's home, and he spent six months in jail. Once he was released, I felt like I was losing him to the streets.

In the meantime, the other sons were using my oldest as an example of what not to be. They wanted more out of life; they saw the crime and the violence, and they wanted something better. They were thirteen and eight, and I also had a new stepson (also eight) who I was raising with my life partner. I now had to protect the boys from their brother and educate them about the world. They felt their brother had become their enemy. "Does he love us? Why is he acting this way?" At this point, his father really had no idea what to do. I truly needed him to be a father, to step up to the plate, but he didn't know what to do. Ultimately, he left everything up to me.

When my older son reached out for help or love, his father pushed him away out of frustration with the son that he had become. It just felt like we were spending so much time on my older son. My son was all over the place, but we still showed lots of love and support for him. We had to put the whole house on lockdown to help him get on track.

I recall one instance where my youngest son could not find his Nintendo DS, and to this day we wonder if my older son had actually taken it and done something with it. Surrounded by the love and support of a strong, loving mate and father figure, we moved again, this time into a single-family home in Will County. My oldest son was now a junior in high school. It was a new environment and far away from bad friends, he was getting good grades, he had made new friends, he was expressing himself, his confidence had increased, and he saw a brighter future.

Then my eldest dropped a bombshell: he and his brother had gotten out of school and gone to visit a young lady. One of the boys kicked the door down and raided her kitchen. She called the police to tell them the situation. My son was taken back to jail, and this time, his brother was with him.

Both my sons went to jail for stealing. The arrest was over a rice crispy treat taken from this young lady's home. My oldest was questioned by the police, hand-cuffed with no notification to his parents, and arrested without a phone call. So, we were concerned about the racial profiling. My problems were being compounded over a senseless situation, and both boys were in the juvenile jail in Joliet. My middle boy spent a month, and the oldest, being a previous offender, spent six months inside.

By the time he got out he was seventeen years old. My other son, who was fourteen, was scared straight, unwilling to ever spend another night in jail. It was just the unfortunate lesson he needed to set his life on the straight and narrow.

My oldest son returned home to Job Corps, too embarrassed to return to high school. His friends had grown up and moved on. There were too many things that he realized he had missed: prom, graduation, and obtaining a driver's license. The shame consumed him. So he went to Job Corps. He completed the program and lived in Indiana for one year.

We had relocated again to a different single-family home. My other sons were doing well: the two youngest were in middle school and heavily involved in sports and played musical instruments. My middle son was an honors student and on the wrestling and soccer teams.

My oldest finally returned home to live with everyone. He noticed that a lot had changed—he didn't have that many friends anymore, and he didn't even have an ID at eighteen years of age. We were finally happy; we had put the past behind us and were so proud of everyone. I promised my oldest son that I would give him a down payment for a car, which I did. Even with that, he was struggling with what to do next. He took the money for the car and went back to Indianapolis. He made a few bad choices once again and, as an adult, he went back to jail; however, this time it was hard time, with adults, for one month. I, on the other hand, had finally completed my bachelor's degree in education and immediately enrolled in graduate school.

Once my oldest son was released, he moved around a bit. At the time, my middle son was away at college at Northern Illinois University, and my oldest thought he would go live with him. I was delighted, having finally completed graduate school with a master's in science education. To my surprise, this is where my oldest son's life turned around. The time spent with his brother, surrounded by an academic atmosphere, inspired him to enroll in college. In the fall of 2017 he graduated with a degree in automotive collision and repair. Faith in God is the secret to my success—and perseverance as a parent has carried me through.

I had always wondered what it would be like to be a member of a larger family, one in which there were at least five or six siblings. I found it intriguing how these families seemed to work together and bond to share experiences, love, and support for one another. From the outside, it always appeared that they had it all figured out. It would always be exciting to see them bonding during the holidays, or sharing in special family moments. I thought that larger families never needed outside friends, because they could provide their own internal friendships. I felt like the parents within these families really had things together, because they seemed to know how to deal with the variety of life's hurdles, as they surely had seen and experienced it all.

Well, looks can be deceiving. Even the most prayerful, loving family has its hurdles in the most unlikely settings and circumstances. This next scenario tells of one family's unique ability to learn to bridge the gap in communicating with the various personalities and styles of its family members. I think you might be surprised by the source of their counsel and learn to lean on nontraditional resources to help your own family find answers in raising your children successfully.

Chapter Six

Spreading the Love with the Five Love Languages

D uring a recent interview, a very good friend shared and intriguing story that is being delivered to you in her own voice. I am a married mother raising four children as a Seventh-day Adventist. The way in which I love and guide our household principles is supported by my faith; however, the biggest source of reference came from an unlikely place. It was actually "*The Five Love Languages*" that brought me closer to my family, which is truly a blessing. I believe that the Lord put it on my heart to reference this tool to reach my children.

In my early parenting years my spouse and I had decided to avoid activity for sports and recreation that fell on the Sabbath, which is Saturday. But we quickly had to rethink our approach, as the conflicts occurred almost routinely. I knew then that I would have to work on the concept of giving my children the freedom of choice that God gives us. They have to live through their own relationship with God. I had to start teaching them that they have choices, and choices have consequences. If that's what you decide to do, that's your choice.

Raising my kids, I teach them all the same thing: I teach them to remember who they are, that they are my child and God's child. This has been my guiding principle. But even with this awesome foundation, I found challenges reaching each one of my children over the years. The moment of reflection that led me to "The Five Love Languages" has truly been rewarding.

In starting out as a parent, my spouse and I both read a book called *The Five Love Languages*; these languages are physical touch, quality time, words of affirmation, acts of service, and gifting. This was the first and only book that allowed us to understand our differences in displaying love as a couple, and it made sense for us to utilize this approach once we had kids to understand their needs and how the approach applies to how they need love and receive love.

Starting with our youngest, who's only four: he's at that stage where he needs hugs and kisses and likes to cuddle and be under his parents. As long as I can offer that to him, he's happy. Our oldest doesn't like physical touch; she prefers intimate quality time, such as that spent watching movies and playing games with just her parents and not the other siblings. This child is a quiet spirit, and this type of quality time brings her out of her shell. I find that she is able to speak freely and openly about things that matter most to her. If I don't give this child that one-on-one time, she doesn't share, and it took time to identify this trait and learn how to meet her needs and show her love. I had tried every single approach to love languages to find what brought satisfaction to her. It took me a while to get in the right frame of mind to try this approach with the love languages, and once I did it wasn't long before I made this discovery. Both the middle children respond well to gifts or rewards—something as small as a piece of gum—to demonstrate that I care about their actions and demonstrate my love for them.

I had tried these separate approaches with each of my four children, and through discovery I learned that they don't appreciate me unless I work within their love language to reach them.

A good example of what I mean was best displayed over the 2015 Christmas holiday. My oldest had asked for a cell phone in the past, and that year we decided to get her one. It was the last big gift she received, and she opened it, said thanks, and moved on with her holiday. I knew then I had to go back to ground zero and refocus on her love language of quality time, because that's how she is best nurtured. It's profound to understand that I need to meet her where she is.

It's natural that you use all the five love languages with all your children, but it's the one that meets them where they are that will create that special bond with each and every one of your children. My family has found this to be the most critical takeaway when working with this resource. Ideally, you could embrace any of the love languages, but it won't make much of an impact if your child isn't being heard and you don't truly understand where they are mentally and psychologically. It's important that you read both their heart and mind to help fill in the blanks. If you are uncertain, it may be best to try all five and keep the one that you and your child respond to the best.

As parents, the best trait we can give to our children is the ability to be comfortable in their own skin and to have a sense of self-worth. In a world that is filled with harsh realities and people who will stand in judgment of one another, it's important for young adults to believe in themselves. It's also equally important for parents to remain supportive of our children as they seek to find themselves. We need to remind ourselves that the world is a cruel place at times, and not everyone will be understanding of our actions, choices, or feelings. As parents, it's our job to instill in our children a level of confidence and pride in the choices they will make and the ability to stand up for what they believe in. Sometimes as an observer it will be challenging to witness, but we have to allow freedom of self-expression. I think this aspect of parenting can become one of the most challenging to master. As parents, we want to shield our children from the cruel world around them. I love the level of support and understanding this next mother displays as she works through several challenging moments of acceptance with both her son and daughter. A true lesson in compassion and tolerance is at the core of her story.

Chapter Seven

Self-Love

Barbara is wonderful mother of two, in this next chapter she shares her own version of how she has taught her children to embrace self-love. I am a married parent with a son who is twenty-two and a daughter who is seventeen. My daughter is very focused and driven; my son, although intelligent, lacks focus and proper time management skills. My son learned a life lesson from grade school when he did not graduate on time with his peers but later graduated with honors; it taught him perseverance.

I try not to put my kids in a box. What works for one may not work for the other. However, the basics are constant: the rules are the rules, no matter if you're a boy or a girl, and I try to be consistent with those things. I try to make them feel whole and give them as much encouragement as possible that they can do all things. However, even with the best encouragement, love, and support, there can still be some hurdles.

For example, my son went away to college, and it didn't initially work out. However, he recently re-enrolled himself and came home with a schedule. I know that a degree helps, but it will not fully determine his future. Could it be a trade? What I know is that whatever he chooses, he will have to work at it. I hope that through this life-learning phase some good will come. However, the jury is still out on his success. As I see the really good friends that my son grew up with, I notice they aren't enrolled in school, so I think maybe it's time for him to pursue a new circle of friends to motivate him and keep him going.

My daughter seems to be more focused, confident, and driven, but I know it does not mean she will be more successful. She is carrying the torch right now, but she, too, may drop it along the way. My goal is for her to learn from any mistakes. I also do my best to remain nonjudgmental of the paths that they choose, even when it involves aspects of life that I may be uncomfortable with, such as relationships and sexuality.

Earlier last year my daughter shared that she was having feelings for the same sex. In this case, her first experience was with a female who was transitioning to become a male, and my daughter began to refer to herself as a pansexual. Although I was shocked and taken aback, I knew how important it would be for me to remain open and allow for positive lines of communication, as I had read the many horror stories of young adults who were not free to live out their truths and either committed suicide or lost all relations with their families. I was determined that this would not be our story. After all, my daughter is the same loving, kind, and intelligent young woman she has always been, it's just that her feelings of affection are different than some of her peers.

Although each day of this journey has been a life-learning experience for me as a parent, as well as her father, we try to keep an open mind. This year, my daughter has moved on from her initial attraction, and as with any young high school relationship, she is now on to other matters of the heart and has found interest in a young lady. Once again, I find myself uncertain and confused about her future, however, I continue to remain supportive and allow for open lines of communication. In a few short months, she will be off to college, and my hope is that she will finally find her true heart's content along with a wonderful college education.

At this point I have every confidence that they both will do well. My prayer is that although it takes some longer than others, they both will find their own level of success. The key will be for me to allow them to live out their truths and to experience life as it unfolds and to continue to support and guide them along the way. I know that everyone does not take the same path to wind up at a similar destination.

Giving birth to children is one of life's true wonders. The birth of a child is the single most wonderful aspect of life. With the birth of a child comes many expectations and a life filled with anticipation for what that child will become. However, from time to time life throws us a few curve balls. Maybe that son or daughter isn't picture perfect, or maybe they are perfect for us. No matter what the revelation, we face these challenges head on. In this next short, we learn what it truly means to be different and so uniquely made that you inspire those around you to dare to be different. We learn how important it can be to step outside our comfort zones and explore uncharted territory to find our own way toward success. We learn what it means to be the same but different. This next chapter is narrated from the perspective of a mother of twins.

Chapter Eight

Deal with the Cards You Are Dealt

Before my twins were born I was in the hospital for two and a half months, and the night before they were born I had decreased fetal movement with the baby on the upper right. The doctor came in the next morning to get me further along and said the baby on the right—my son—needed to be taken immediately. He stayed in the hospital two weeks, and I pumped and took milk back weekly. Three months later, I noticed decreased ability to feed, and he was stiff in my arms. Although I was taking him in to the doctor regularly, my primary doctor was absent when I went for a routine visit, and I had a chance encounter with a different doctor. This new doctor saw something we had not, and he decided to run some additional tests. Being a doctor myself, I decided to get a head scan; it showed hydrocephalus, and cerebral palsy was diagnosed. When you have these concerns, early detection and frequent second opinions are critical.

As a family, we had to learn to deal with the differences, but one cannot crawl forever. The Department of Child and Family Services was brought in because my son suffered a fall and broke his big bone in his thigh. Even as a doctor, I didn't know that patients with cerebral palsy injuries required different areas of care for recovery.

As time moved on, we learned to adjust and deal with the challenges of raising a child with a disability. We learned to lean on one another for support and encouragement and to support one another as a team.

I thought that everything was great and that nobody had any complaints, however, my eyes were opened when I read a senior year essay where my daughter referred to herself as a nurse to her twin brother. But she also pointed out she never wanted it to be any other way. Her love for her brother was not an extra load. However, could I have been wrong? Maybe I had not taken her feelings into account.

What I made certain to do was to ensure that both kids were well adjusted. I always spoke to the benefits of the teens having what they needed, never referencing that there was a special one. I think this resonated with my son the most, as he never has looked at himself as having a disability. He always planned for the same activities and level of success as his peers who did not have disabilities.

As a result, I found myself always looking for the best schools. My son went to a school called Skinner.

When the children were old enough for high school, we didn't have enough money to send them to private school, and our educational system did not allow them to go to the same school. This was divine intervention and a true blessing, because they both finally got their independence. My daughter no longer had to carry my son's bags, and my son was allowed to express his independence. The time apart during the day made them appreciate one another in ways that were unimaginable. As time moved on and it was time for college, things went full circle. Both kids had been accepted to different schools, but they had one in common. It was yet another blessing to know that they would be there for one another on the same campus and proudly graduate together.

I can honestly say that the twins are well adjusted, partially due to their parents. Although they lived in a split household, they have been able to provide a loving home and coparent effectively for their greater good. I learned patience, and it made us stronger as a unit. I felt needed and helpful. I taught my son to seek the help he needs, because not everyone can read minds. As I've said earlier, my son has never seen himself as a person with disabilities. His independence breaks down the barriers of difference.

Going to the right school is critical. Choosing his school made a real difference, because even though his school was not a school for the disabled, it offered access to students who were, which allowed him to accept that he was not alone. My daughter was able to break away, have fun, and come home and be a friend to her brother.

It's awesome to witness how the twins have built lifelong friendships. I guess, in the end, I learned that they are indeed the same but different. They will both conquer life's challenges because they have mastered dealing with the cards they have been dealt.

From the day our children are born we have a master plan for them. We know which schools we want them to attend—moving from grade school to middle school, then high school and on to college. Make no mistake; we know what we want our offspring to become later in life. And it's not surprising that we even have ideas about the type of person we would like them to marry. We may never speak about this psychological plan, but it's there, residing in the back of our minds. Soon after, we proceed to execute this plan connecting the dots with participation in athletic, social, and academic activities. We begin our journey of mixing and mingling with various social and community based organizations in an effort to mold a champion! But then, as life would have it, we get hit with the curve ball. The curve ball is the reality that our children somehow have their own plans that totally deviate from what we had in mind. It's during this time that we as parents must face this truth head on and understand that this is the right course of action, as it's the course that leads them toward self-awareness. Self-awareness is the conscious knowledge of one's own character, feelings, motives, and desires. Once a young adult has a firm hold on their own desires, there is nothing that can stop them from reaching their goals and fulfilling their own dreams. Learn in this next mothers own voice how she kept a level head and open mind to be receptive of a plan that was totally not her own.

Chapter Nine

Living Your Own Dreams

A t the age of twenty-eight, I was a single mom. I was living with my daughter's father, and when I got pregnant I knew that I wanted to have my daughter. I never once contemplated not having her. All kinds of emotions and thoughts went through my mind: Would I be a good mother? I knew right away that her father would not be an active participant in her life. Two years after she was born, we were on our own, and he was in jail. The support of family is what got us through her early life. The saying "it takes a village" is true; the village helped me to go back to school and obtain a bachelor's degree. This village allowed me to grow up, as well as raise my daughter.

It was a tough journey, but nothing has caused us to miss a beat with anything I wanted to do in our lives. I knew that I wanted to expose my daughter to extra-curricular activities—tap, ballet, and modeling—at an early age. She began violin and tennis at age three. I joined an organization for women of color to expose myself to likeminded mothers who wanted the same things for their children. This organization added an additional village to our existing village. The inspiration from this group of likeminded mothers was encouraging for more than ten years.

During this time, my daughter became friends with people that we both have maintained relations with, even after she graduated. I have relied on this village to help in raising my daughter.

Who is my daughter? The attributes that stick out the most are her independence and strength of will. I remember when she was younger and she would call me at work and tell me her weekend plans. She would have a great-aunt pick her up on a Friday evening, then have her grandmother take her to activities, and on Sunday she would have that same aunt take her home to prepare for the next week. The chauffer and financial backing would be lined up from Friday to Sunday to execute her well-laid plans.

Thinking about being independent and being strong willed: As any parent, you have goals and dreams laid out for your child. You put them in the best preschools and the top high schools, and the scholarships come in and you think they are going to do this or that. And for the most part my daughter followed my plan, until later in high school when she became somewhat resistant. In one instance I recall, she took it upon herself to run for teen youth vice president of Jack and Jill of

America—and won—and then she was elected as teen president. I was a happy mom. My plans seemed to be coming into fruition; she was a leader who would take control.

Then she went to college, and she could not seem to figure out her niche in life. As a mother, I told her what she was good at and what things I thought would be best for her. Two years went by and lots of money was spent and dollars were adding up. We needed to figure this out.

My daughter had a surprise for me; she had figured this out for herself. We had planned to look for apartments in her second year of college and move her into her own apartment for her third year of college. That Tuesday of finals weeks, she called me.

"I will be home after finals," she said.

I said, "Are you coming home for the summer?"

"Mom, I'm coming home tomorrow."

She paused. I was thinking, "Oh, hell no," just before the silence was broken.

"Mom, I don't want to disappoint anyone, but I want to come home and I want to cook."

At that moment, I realized my plan was not her plan at all, and I had to let it go.

When she started to say that she was afraid of disappointing everyone, I knew that I had to tell her we would support her in anything that she wanted to do. I told her, "This is your plan, and you will have to figure this out." And, she did just that. She reached out to people in her field to explore her options—and these were people that I trusted to give her sound advice. She came home, enrolled in culinary school, graduated, and has been living her own dream of running a successful catering business ever since.

As a mother or father, you think that you are going to parent in a certain way before you give birth, but I've learned that you have to remain flexible. A critical aspect of parenting is getting to know your child first, along with accepting who they are. Once you truly know your child, it's easy to incorporate a parenting style. The one-size-fits-all parenting approach is always a pathway to heartache. Meet one family that found out the hard way that each child has a unique set of needs that often require a different approach to support. In this next chapter I will take you on this journey.

Chapter Ten

No Comparison

Cheryl had a boy and a girl who were polar opposites. Her son James was a lively, humorous, 6 foot 3 nonathletic male who had tons of charisma and charm. At first encounter, he was always the life of the party. James had the gift of gab and easily made many friends. Oftentimes his humor was also his biggest vice. James took life very lightly, as he was easily distracted and ready to entertain his peers. These personality traits eventually made for a bad recipe in the classroom, and sometimes he was an unpopular student with his teachers. Cheryl always told me that she was concerned about James the most because he really didn't take his education as seriously as she preferred. She worried if he would be true college material if he didn't perform well in high school.

In contrast, Cheryl had a college freshman named Bria who had always exceeded her academic expectations. At every step of the road Bria had pleased her mother with the honor roll, high test scores, and a laser focus on outperforming her peers. Bria was at the top of her class and really enjoyed her high school career as she played a major role in the success of her high school volleyball team and tested well as she prepared for college.

I can recall that Cheryl never planned to institute a curfew with the kids, because she had such a strong level of trust when raising Bria. As the oldest, Bria had never been told when to come home. But for James, the rules seemed to have changed. He began to hang out with friends, and the feeling was that he may not come home for days without the added reinforcement of the curfew.

As far as trust, she raised them to be honest and open. Cheryl knew that with her daughter, she had someone who was very goal oriented, and she wouldn't allow anything to take her off her path. Cheryl always thought that her oldest would even get a scholarship for athletics or academia, and she was correct, as she did receive a full-ride scholarship.

Her son, however, talked around the truth. He wasn't a liar, but Cheryl had a different level of trust with him.

So, after a very successful high school experience with Bria, Cheryl decided the same high school would be the best fit for a successful outcome for James. I can recall sharing with Cheryl my philosophy on keeping an open mind about high school and not choosing a school simply out of convenience, but finding a school that would support the whole child and his approach to learning. I thought a performing arts high school might be the right approach. However, like many parents, Cheryl felt like that atmosphere did not have enough structure and academic resources for a high school student who needed to prepare for college, so the choice was made to send James to the same high school that Bria had attended.

The first few weeks were brutal. James was one of only a handful of minority students, and it seemed that he always found himself in trouble where trouble did not exist. The academic pressure of attending one of the top-ranking high schools in the state did not help James with his lackluster attitude toward studying. I could always see beyond the silly and playful James into a young, creative mind that seemed to be ready to explode with talents that remained hidden in the restricted environment, where no one seemed to care about cultivating the talents that laid within. It appeared that even the faculty were disappointed in his desire not to take up a sport like basketball, considering his tremendous height. James seemed to be falling through the cracks. Finally, everything came to a head when James was suspended for trying to break up a fight; he even was injured in the process. I can recall Cheryl boiling with anger that her son had such a large bruise and was being penalized while his peers were able to walk away with just a warning. Was it that the faculty was fed up with James and his classroom follies, or were they simply being racially prejudiced? I guess we will never know. Thankfully, it was just a few days before summer break, and Cheryl decided to transfer James into a new school that she had heard so many great things about. It wasn't the fancy top-ranking school, but it was indeed a school where James felt he may finally have an opportunity to soar. Bria could not believe what she was witnessing. After all, who would want to attend a school so far away from home in an urban area away from everything they had ever known?

From the first month of school we could see the change; it was almost instant. James was prospering like a seed in fresh soil. He made a total turnaround with his academics, and fears about leaving old friends were made void by the numerous new buddies he was hanging out with each week. James had become the apple of many teachers' eyes.

Cheryl told me that the one thing that she always wanted as a mother was to expose her kids to the best schools, but the biggest eye opener was that the fifth-ranked high school in the state simply was not the best fit for her son. Cheryl learned that the best schools are more than national rankings and even moved far beyond academics. The ability to look beyond her prior experience with her daughter demonstrated that one size really

was not for all, and that in parenting you can never
really compare.

I cautioned myself as I decided to write about this next tragedy, as it really brings up a lot of hurtful memories, but I think that it also demonstrates the essence of true healing, bonding, resilience, and perseverance when raising a child. I trust that this story of triumph and pain will lead to the healing of others who may have experienced devastation, and that they will go on with life and prosper in the same way that this family has been able to heal and move mountains. In order to fully protect the privacy of this story's participants, various details have been altered, but the foundation of the story remains true to the source.

Chapter Eleven

Healing from the Horror: A Mother's Love

You can never judge a book by its cover. If you were to look at this mother and son duo, you would never imagine the life tragedy that she had to endure to get to the happy space she is in today. Some eighteen years ago, Margaret was a happy mother of two loving daughters. Today, they would be twenty-two and twenty-four. Mary and Monica were the apple of their mother's eye. Both girls were filled with such joy and laughter and were true kindred spirits with their mother.

Margaret was faced with going through a divorce, which left her and her former spouse dividing their time with the girls between the two of them. It wasn't odd when her ex-husband told her that he would be taking the girls to a family reunion in Arkansas. As she packed the girls for their trip, I'm certain she never imagined that it was the last time she would see them.

While at work, Margaret got the call that no mother ever wants to receive. It was the coroner asking her to come and identify two bodies they believed to be her children. Sad to say, the burned bodies were, indeed, those of her two precious jewels.

Margaret was a lost soul for quite some time, until she began to truly lean on the Lord in her church home. As time moved on, so did Margaret. She found love again, and that led to the birth of her miracle son. This son was the saving grace that gave Margret hope and new life after losing her daughters many years prior. Margaret was determined to raise this son in the eyes of the Lord with a strong foundation of Christian principles and moral beliefs. The church had become the sole source of her salvation.

As her son, Marcus, was growing up, he became frustrated with so much time spent away from friends and focused on the church. His mother became really protective of the friends he kept and the places he went. She truly wanted the best for her son and could not accept anything less; he was her one and only child, and her hopes and dreams for their entire family rested upon his success and progress.

I can recall her sharing that he had become rebellious and had fallen in line with a bad crowd of young folks who were encouraging him to explore new things that would only lead him down the wrong path. Her only recourse was to stay on him and deny his ability to go most places. Things like dates, prom, and visits to certain friends' homes were prohibited. Like any young teenager, Marcus began to sneak around to do the things that he wanted to do.

It was hard to witness the pair growing apart when I knew that they both needed each other so much. I decided to have a chat with Marcus. He was indeed spiraling out of control. However, I was surprised to learn that Marcus, who was wise beyond his years, had a true soft spot in his heart for his mother. He knew that he was her miracle baby and that she was protesting because she feared losing him to adulthood. We spoke about what it would mean for her to experience life without him, and those thoughts seemed to frighten him.

When it was time for college, Marcus was ready to spread his wings. He had become far more focused on academics in his senior year than he was for all the three years he spent in high school, because he was concerned about not getting into college. It turned out that his mother had been correct all those years, and Marcus had been wasting valuable time that could have been better spent improving his grades. However, as any good mother, she helped Marcus find his way and apply to schools, several of which accepted him. Marcus now had options, and his mother was finally able to allow him to Grow and Go, and with the encouragement, love, and support of her church, family, and friends, she knew that it was finally okay to let go.

When Marcus sent me their pictures from college drop off, I could see the joy and pride in both their faces. Margaret had come a long way, she was sad to give her son to the world but proud to see him prepared to take on the tasks at hand. He was indeed a winner! She knew that all the love, support, and Christian values that she had poured into him over the years would guide and protect him as he moved forward in his own life.

I think the true moral to this story is to understand that smothering a child may come from many places of emotional concern, but with patience and prayer we can overcome the urge to stifle growth and the natural progression from childhood to adulthood. Someone on the outside looking in might think that this mother is over the top and too sheltering, but until you've walked a mile in her shoes it simply will never make sense.

This next chapter is about a young woman who was able to conquer the stigma of teen pregnancy with the love and support of family told from my own personal encounter. Sometimes we find ourselves in these precarious situations and want to give up. Some decide that the road ahead is too rough to travel, and they wind up on welfare or they wind up back at home living with their family. I think it's important to understand and know that this does not have to be our destiny, nor does it have to be the destiny of our children. History doesn't always repeat itself, but when it does and our children have a wonderful road map to follow, the journey is always a lot easier. In this next chapter, learn how I was blessed to witness such an encounter.

Chapter Twelve

I Didn't
Raise a Monster

In high school, I had the pleasure of making the acquaintance of a family with both the mother and father still present. It was somewhat of an anomaly for the time, because many families had broken marriages with single moms. It was refreshing to witness, and this family became a second family to my own. As the only girl in the house, my girlfriend was the apple of everyone's eye in this family. She was a bright ball of fire, always meeting everyone with her competitive wit and drive to become a doctor.

During this time, our families had chosen to send us to Catholic school. We followed this path from grade school up until the end of high school. While in high school, I introduced my friend to the man who would become the father of her child. He was Hispanic with a fun-loving, entrepreneurial personality, and she was African-American with a very serious and focused outlook on life. I was always the matchmaker in my bunch, and I established the acquaintance of this unlikely pairing. As the school year went on the relationship prospered, and my friend became pregnant in our senior year of high school. It was taboo for the time—especially in a Catholic school environment. I can recall being so worried about what the future would hold for my friend; I watched from the sidelines as the school denied her the ability to attend prom and graduation. As time went on, we graduated and went our separate ways. My friend, with the love and support of her family, took her son with her as she went away to college. She was determined to succeed and not allow her parents to become his parents.

Personally, she always knew that she would be a nurturer. Her own brother was some six years younger than she was, and she descended like an eagle to help parent him. She had always been that person. Yet, she never thought that she would be a teenage mom.

I can recall her sharing that she never thought she could love someone as much as she loved her child. She had him at seventeen, and it was simply instinctive. As a competitive person Cheryl always wanted so much out of life, it was phenomenal to witness. Her decisions did not align with the path that her parents had planned for her, as she had become an adult really early, but she prospered. It was she and her son against the world.

She was thankful for him, as he gave her tunnel vision. She wanted to give him the best possible life; she didn't care what other people thought. She admired her friends' freedom from afar as they engaged in other aspects of young life, but it didn't affect her drive to succeed. She had a plan, and no one would take her off course.

I can recall her sharing, "My son was a great kid and I had fun raising him, even though I was nineteen and he was two. The hard part was not providing shelter, food, or even an education; it is the emotional aspect that was the challenge. You never want your child to be hurt or in pain, but as a parent, I believe that I needed to teach him right from wrong. I didn't want to do it, but I had to. I had no intent to raise a monster. But there was still so much I didn't have control over."

The most difficult stage for my friend came when her son was eleven years old. This was the tween stage of life, and he was starting to look like a young man. They were in a store and he walked away, doing his thing, and all of a sudden he came over to her, appearing shaken. This man had approached him and asked him why was he there and what was he doing. My friend realized people were starting to see him not as this cute little kid but an intimidating young black man. Raising a young African-American man would be no joke. That was her first wake-up call; she knew then that this would not be easy. She could not protect him from everything. As a single mom, she was somewhat of a control freak, and she was grateful that she did not need anyone else's approval in how she would raise him. It was her word, and he had to live with it. There was no democracy; this was a dictatorship. However, she was a good listener. She was the queen without a king. He would later appreciate it when he became a father of his own child.

Things went really well until he turned seventeen. My friend's son became tired of following her way and really wanted to express and become himself. He was no longer a baby, and he would be who he wanted to be. It was hard for her to embrace, but her way did not work for him. She shared that "I didn't throw my hands up and give up, but it was indeed a struggle, being a female raising a male who was trying to become a man. We never understood that there was no tag team." Even now, he has told her that he has great respect for her as a mother.

Her own father, whom they called Poppie, had become a role model for him. But at the end of the day, his grandfather was not his father. It had nothing to do with her parenting; it was the missing link. That struggle and turmoil were there because he wanted his own father, and his selfish, all-consuming attitude was not in line with those who loved him. I think everyone would have liked to throw up their middle finger—but they couldn't. His mother was losing sleep, and his decision-making was off. My friend tried to pull his father in, but he wasn't dependable and Cheryl didn't respect his decision-making. It was indeed an eye-opener when I learned from her son's father, "You have to remember, he's half me." It was in that very moment that she came to terms with her son and the man he would be. At the end of the day, we want our children to live a life grander or greater than ours—a life with less pain—but it's their choice to make.

I can recall that the son started going to proms and dances earlier than most. And more than a few girls' mothers would stand in judgment of him, and my friend would think to herself, "Huh, they are lucky ones." Her son would say, "You raised me, but I am not a replica of you. You tell me to be myself, but what you're really saying is *be like me*."

She knew he would never be the A student she was, but he would do fine. In watching her, I found that her patience level was not good with her own child and her expectations were much too high. A tag or title on the door was not his style; he was happiest being able to work as a free spirit and entrepreneur. Being the CEO of his own company was more like his dad; he was always the real risk taker.

Being someone's parent forces you to reflect on who you are. My friend confided in me that the reason she wasn't much of a risk taker was because she was a single parent. Single parents can't afford to take risks when they have no one to fall back on. She became fearful instead of fearless. In contrast, her son looked at everything with a positive perspective and became open to the risky days ahead.

At twenty-three years old, her son became a father. She found out when during a visit my friend and her son were laughing and talking, and he said, "Mom, I have something that I wanted to talk to you about." Her heart raced. He told her, "I am going to be a father." The first thing she said was, "Son, you're so young!" And her first thought was, "Now I have someone else to worry about." But time would pass and nature would take its course and work things out one day at a time.

He is now twenty-eight, and when it comes to being a grandparent, my friend's defining moment with her son was when she, too, experienced her grandchild coming into this world. She witnessed her son become a father, tears running down his face. That love that she could not describe had now been experienced by her own son. She was still feeling fantastic, having experienced the cycle of life. She told me she recalls feeling bad about it, but she began to laugh when she reminded herself of her famous words: "Enjoy it while you can, son, and pray you don't raise a monster."

Chapter Thirteen

Looking for the Wow

As parents, we are always looking for the "Wow!" We find ourselves constantly seeking opportunities to showcase our children's strengths and capabilities. We want that stand-out opportunity that lets the world know that we have accomplished our goal. However, as we are seeking the wow, we need to ask ourselves, are we so caught up with the idea of success that we neglect the milestones that help our young truly Grow and Go?

I know I've been guilty of this aspect of parenting too many times to count. From the day my girls were born I placed the highest level of expectations on both of them. I've always been great at identifying a person's true talents, and once I honed in on these strengths within my daughters I immediately set out on my own personal mission to help them reach the goal. I had never really taken into account what they loved, I just pushed forward with what I knew they could achieve. For a long time, this worked in my favor. When children are young, they go along with most things that we ask of them without question. It's when they get older that they challenge the status quo. This is indeed the reality for us.

When she was three years old I knew my oldest was a fantastic athlete. I could also see that she was out-spoken, she had a thirst for knowledge, and she loved to draw. Right away I capitalized on her athletic talents by enrolling her in gymnastics, track, basketball, and later golf. My hope was that she would find a home within one of these sports and develop her skills well enough to grant her an athletic scholarship. Several months into gymnastics, as she became more skilled, the pressure to perform increased so much that she asked to give it up. I was shocked and, I must admit, disappointed, because her Olympic gold medalist instructors had repeatedly reinforced that she had a gymnast's body and was made for "competition." No matter how many attempts I made, she had lost enthusiasm.

Then came track. She was the smallest but always the fastest, moving at lightning speed with an awk-ward form and a dainty hand posture. She won more than a few initial competitions, but then we stepped up our game and acquired a track coach. Once again, this was my attempt to perfect her craft. The practices were almost daily, and the coach's commitment expectations for her team were unwavering. As we embarked upon many restless, long nights of practice, homework, and late-night dinners, I saw the light begin to dim, and it wasn't long until it happened again. "Mom, I'm tired of track, it's just not for me."

As I became frustrated, I can recall my spouse saying, "It's my turn. What about basketball?" I can't say that I was excited, because I knew little to nothing about the sport. I just knew it wasn't the traditional lady-like sport that I was accustomed to. However, it turned out to be the one that stuck. From grade school into sophomore year of high school, basketball had become our fan favorite. My daughter was the starting point guard and was a delight to watch as she averaged twenty-two points a game. I thought surely this would be our ticket to a free ride to college. But just as I began to embrace the sport and could finally call a play, it happened again. The high school coach was dealing with far more competitive teams, and as a result his demands of his players had become far more intense. Meanwhile, homework and class work were becoming more challenging. The ability to balance the two became a fierce battle until one day midseason she asked to give it up. I was more than disappointed, and I think my husband was about to lose it. In a house full of hormones, my daughter's love of sports and basketball had become his only refuge. Indeed, we were disappointed.

I can recall that it was that summer during a chance encounter with her father that she found a new love in golf. As a southpaw, she seemed to hold a unique advantage and had a keen eye for precision on the course. Her team coach and captain supported the idea of her applying for the Chick Evans Golf Caddy Scholarship, as she truly had an eye for the game. But just as she became great at the sport, she grew tired of the all-day tournaments and daily practices and gave it up before graduating. I'd ask myself how someone so great at so many sports could just walk away. Was it a fear of competition? Was it a fear of putting in hard work? Was it merely a growth process where you continue to try things out until you find a real home?

When my mind wasn't on her physical strengths, I focused on her creative capabilities. I remember the first day that a Judy Blume illustrator came to visit her grade school and viewed a portfolio that my daughter had created to share with her. It was during this time that I received the note that every parent hopes to receive. It read, "You have a true gift here. Be sure to cultivate it. Enroll her in formal classes ASAP. What an amazing talent." I was blown away and didn't let any wind get under my feet; I signed her up with the best at the Art Institute of Chicago. While creative art was fun, we expanded to architecture. I had her future all planned out in my mind. She would attend Cooper Union in New York City for free and go on to work at one of the top architectural firms.

Fast forward to years later, she is now in college with a dual major in clinical health leadership & management and business. I must say that for a college sophomore she has more career-shadowing experience than any of her peers. Over three hundred hours working in various hospital settings has given her amazing exposure. I'll admit I never saw her as the clinical type. But the feedback has always been that she has a natural gift when working with people, specifically pediatric and geriatric populations. Her most enjoyable moments have been working as a physical therapy intern supporting athletes in their therapy. It seems as though the athlete in her never went away but found a new purpose. Her passion and dedication for the field has grown so much that she has chosen to open up her own therapy center for athletes to receive quality patient therapy. To hear her speak about her patient experiences is to witness true passion for her craft. This summer she has plans to intern with one of the major sporting teams to explore their therapy programs and business marketing strategies. I have no doubt she will find the experience rewarding.

That was my oldest. It's a totally different ball game for my youngest. My youngest came into this world as a silent storm, as I like to call her. She never really has been a talker. Even at birth she didn't cry on demand—it occurred with some effort. Because she was a silent child, I always took that to mean she was shy. And because I thought she was shy, I always felt compelled to step in and lend a helping hand with making friends, planning outings, or signing her up for things I thought she might enjoy. All the while, all I could ever catch her doing was journaling these life events. To that end, we would sign up for tennis, volleyball, swimming, and fashion design classes. Though I did these things, identifying her true talent was a bit more of a challenge. With her silence, it made it tough to know what really moved her. So she tried tennis, and all I can say is that the ball would be searching for the racket nearly every swing. Tennis was not her friend, so without much hesitation she freely gave it up. During a summer vacation, we discovered that both girls were at a disadvantage with not knowing how to swim. So, as soon as we hit stateside, we signed up. I'm not sure if it was the class or the instructor himself, but both girls became little fish. However, my youngest seemed to embrace this sport the most. Her instructor told us on multiple occasions that she had the best form he'd ever seen. So, for five years, straight into high school, this became her sport. I watched her challenge herself to be the best she could be week after week. I just knew that with her vast awards along the way, this would be a college tuition bonus. But, to my surprise, she decided to give it up without warning.

Then came volleyball, and once again my spouse had found a new hobby with being a team coach. Even through the frustration of dealing with various parental personalities and varying skill levels of the players, he enjoyed the bonding time. Tennis seemed to be a fun sport for this daughter, but it was just a fun hobby, nothing to build a college career upon. As time stood still, my daughter picked up a few hobbies like photography, and she even took a few classes at the Art Institute of Chicago with her sister, where she found a love in fashion design. For a while, I thought, "This is it." I helped her trademark a business name and website, and she participated in a showcase fashion show to launch her brand. This was it! I just knew it. But once again, I was wrong. I became frustrated and disappointed by the lack of stability in her pursuit of her passions.

All the while she would lock herself in her room, going through ledger book after ledger book, journaling and writing short stories. It became impossible to keep a blank pad and paper around the house. Then, as fate would have it, my silent sister got in trouble for passing notes during class. When the teacher took the note and read it, she was appalled at the language but amazed by the writing talent. She reached out to complain and praise. I did what every parent dreads. I invaded my daughter's privacy by grabbing one of her many journals to see what all the fuss was about. I could not believe my eyes. I had been searching for the gift, and the gift had been before me all along. As any good mother would do, I networked to give her an opportunity of a lifetime to freelance for a local teen magazine. Through this experience my daughter has become a published author and editor, and it has placed her in the position to intern for one of the top advertising firms in the country as a PR specialist, all before attending her first year of college. As I watched her during her final summer presentation at the firm, I found I could barely recognize my "silent storm." It has become clear to me that her silence gave her the opportunity to find her voice.

As somewhat of a "smother mother," I had made it my goal to identify the life plans for my children. I had seen the gifts but missed how they should best be applied. While I was looking for the *WOW*, the wow was sitting right in front of me. As a parent, my pearl of wisdom is to allow your children to be exposed to many aspects of life but not feel compelled to commit so soon, as life is about trying new things and finding a real purpose and passion to make it a career. The forced pauses or the planned stops are the necessary milestones that will aid in their growth process to ensure that once they leave the nest they will indeed be ready to Grow and Go for good.

Every aspect of these journeys is about struggles that we all may face from being over-protective; having unrealistic expectations; trying to make our children's lives our lives; not knowing how to love; wanting to give up when our children fail too often; comparing our kids to others; sheltering them from the storms of life; using our children as excuses for our own insecurities, fear of failure, fear of the unknown, and fear of disappointment; and the list goes on and on.

Hearing the stories from these families should help to shed light on a few common threads that many of us have or will experience. However, it's what we do with this information that will help us raise a true winner. Ask yourself, which story did you identify with the most? Is their story your story? How would you handle things? Did you offer the proper support in your situation, or could you have handled it better? These are the thought-provoking questions that we all must face to help our children Grow and Go.

The Grow and Go® Theory

You've seen the term Grow and Go® thrown out more than a few times as you have been reading, and I'd like to shed some light as to what this really means.

The Grow and Go® theory, as I like to call it, is a term of endearment that I have used for years to help express my desire to have parents take a step back in their parenting and release the reins to allow their children to become more independent thinkers. The theory rests in the fact that as parents we want to one day see our children grow up and move out on their own and be successful, that is, a winner. Sound familiar? Well, the problem is that not everyone is easily able to allow this theory to move into action, myself included. If you think you are a good mom or dad, you probably want to help guide your child's decision-making process so that they can avoid some of the mistakes you have witnessed or mistakes you may have made. Guess what? That's admirable, but it's also very crippling. Oftentimes, our attempt to support or help our children is actually thinking for them or doing so much of the work ourselves that our children fail to learn the life lesson we mean to teach them to further their growth process. I hope this book has enlightened you and inspires and guides parents with young adults with successfully navigating "this thing called life" (Prince and the Revolution, "Let's Go Crazy," *Purple Rain*).

The Magic

Steps

After five years of supporting 350 students with their college and career planning, I managed to create a road map to success that I like to refer to as the Magic Steps. The Magic Steps are my tips for successfully raising a winner and helping them navigate their life. These steps may not seem like much, but if you reinforce their importance, you can't go wrong.

From the instant your child learns to speak, cultivate an environment of public speaking opportunities. Encourage them to speak in church, pray during dinner, read aloud, and take on leadership roles in athletics and extracurricular activities. No matter what opportunity you decide to utilize as your disguise, be certain to create confident public speakers. "Why?" you might ask. Well, a confident speaker is bound to be more successful in interviews, be more self-confident, and present their best self to the world.

Instill in your child an attitude of gratitude. Little things like sending thank you cards will go a long way. It's these little things that will ensure that someone other than a parent views your child as appreciative.

Encourage your child to become a giver, not a taker, by ensuring that they know the importance of giving back. Demonstrate by donating time on a routine basis to things like feeding the homeless, spending time with the elderly, and participating in toy drives and disaster relief efforts. It's important as an adult that we remain humble and understand that for those whom much is given, much is required. If children learn this trait in their youth, they will be more likely to embody it as an adult.

Help your child live and breathe within a circle of five. The five closest people to your child need to be as smart as they are—or smarter. They should help to motivate, encourage, and stimulate your child's growth. These individuals need to enhance your child's knowledge and foster their character. Everyone has at least one exception, or one person who doesn't fully meet these friendship expectations. However, they, too, should bring value, emotionally, socially, or psychologically.

Teach your child to network from the day they first start school. Stay connected with someone every step of the way by reaching back just to say hello. Always be willing to meet and greet new faces at school, at church, and at play. No matter what the occasion, encourage them to be confident with introducing themselves so that people can place a face with a name. This technique will promote a lifelong ability to navigate the world and open many doors that otherwise might remain closed.

With the purchase of their first phone, demand that your child creates a professional voice-mail message. A good first impression can go a long way. Sometimes they won't get second chances, so encourage them to get it right the first time. Trust me, this is a technique that will help them stand out from their peers.

Encourage your child to always greet new people by sharing something interesting or intriguing about themselves; people who are interesting are rarely forgotten.

Prepare your child early and often for every phase of life. In grade school, start planning for high school. In high school, start preparing for college. In college, prepare for future careers and independence. For example, in grade school, have your child speak with high school students about their workload and expectations, and take them to high school games or events so that they get comfortable with the next phase of life before it hits them. Start visiting colleges as early as freshman year. It's not about selecting schools at this point; it's more about allowing them to see where they are going and what's required to get there. Students that know more, do more.

In the summer of their junior year of high school, help them begin the college application process;

they should request all the necessary letters of recommendation, develop a working resume, and work on an open-ended college essay and personal statement. If they get these things out of the way before schools starts senior year, they can beat the mad rush, apply before their peers, and be accepted early so that they can focus on acquiring scholarships and enjoy a stress-free senior year.

Encourage your child to get a job or volunteer for an internship in their specific field of interest. Local fast-food chains and grocery stores are cool, but they won't help your child fully understand their career choice or give them a cutting edge once they graduate. A graduate with real-world industry experience will always command a higher salary than an entry-level candidate with none.

Help your child choose a college rather than allowing a college to choose them. This means identifying a school that they would love to attend if accepted. This college should support their academic major and maintain programming to support their long-term career aspirations. Let your child know that if they prepare early and often, they will give themselves many opportunities to explore. These actions will permit them to attend a school they want to go to versus one that they have to go to. Become a proponent of cultivating home-grown talent. The communities that we grow up in are the communities that often need us the most, so help your child feel good about attending a college in their own neck of the woods.

You made it! You finally raised a winner.

ACKNOWLEDGMENTS

I am indebted to a host of professionals who have influenced my thinking, supported my programming, embraced the students I serve, and showered my "winners" with tons of love and support. Among these are Sylvia Nelson Jordan of the CPS Academic Competitions, Na-Tae' Thompson and Deanna Sherman of *True Star Magazine*, Leo Burnett, Athletico, Ms. Muliyani of Laren Montessori School, the FBI, Sean and Karen Boston, Patrick Elmore of Mizzou Admissions, John Ambrose and Adam Davis of Michigan State University, Buzz Burnam of the University of Kentucky, Sauvik Goswami of The University of Iowa, Jenny Sawyer of the University of Louisville, Dr. Nichole Butler-Mooyoung, Dr. Shelanda Bobbitt Hayes, Dr. Shelly Gill, Dr. Brandon O'Neil, Dr. Francine Pearce, Justin Baker of the Milwaukee Bucks, Dr. Angela Gordon, Argonne National Labs, Julie Wiggins Stratton, Marki Lemons, Barbara Bates, Spencer Leak Jr., Lanae Davis, Toya Woullard, Michael Cathey, and Melvin Flowers. Last, and most importantly, I want to express my gratitude to my brother, Chris Clark, and my spouse, Andre' Crittle, for stepping up to support every endeavor without hesitation.

About Our Contributors

Jaren Holden, aka Digital Jay, offers a vast array of photographic portrait expressions. Utilizing all-natural landscapes as his canvas, he enjoys creating artistic portraits that can be showcased as genuine works of art. His photography utilizes nature's resources as their own special effects to bring every portrait to life. Whether his subject is an entertainer, athlete, bride or groom, graduate, or family, it's his goal to take his clients on an artistic journey that incorporates digital graphic artistry and real life through every lens. His unique process of visual communication is best expressed through photography and illustration that is made available to his clients in both print and digital imagery. Jaren is a student at Beloit College in Wisconsin. Jaren is responsible for the graphic enhancements on the back cover and internal photos of *Raising A Winner*.

Nia Pennington is a creative mastermind. She is an illustrator, painter, and graphic artist, as well as a student at the University of Kentucky majoring in integrated strategic communication with an art studio minor. Nia brings every original artist canvas to life. Nia is the principal illustrator on the *Raising A Winner* national book cover.

Kayla Crittle is an independent freelance media maven. At the ripe age of eighteen she is a multi-published author, having worked for local *True Star Magazine* as both an editor and a freelance journalist. She has been the voice-over for regional syndicated commercials for clients such as State Farm and True Star, and she is the recipient of the prestigious Leo Burnett Vision Internship. Kayla is also a student at the University of Kentucky majoring in integrated strategic communication with a public relations specialization and a minor in journalism. Kayla is the author of the forward in *Raising A Winner*.

Kai Crittle is the owner and operator of KEC, Inc., aka Keep Everything Creative Communications, which maintains an emphasis on sports and healthcare communication related opportunities. Kai has over five hundred internship service hours and expertise supporting healthcare and sporting organizations. Kai is a student at the University of Kentucky majoring in human communication and minoring in community leadership & development. Kai is responsible for the quote on the cover of the *Raising A Winner* book cover.

Q & A

How did you come up with the title?

Back in 2002 when I opened my first business called The Bookwork, I hired a team of twenty-five high school students from Marian Catholic High School and Homewood Flossmoor High School, and each of these individuals exceeded every expectation I could imagine as a parent and business owner. Each student had the highest level of academic accolades, commitment, and dedication to their work. As time has gone on and they all have become successful adults, I realized that they represented the best of what we as parents would like to call winners, so I decided that this would become the foundation of the book along with its title.

What's your favorite short, and why?

"Comfort Buddy" is my favorite story simply because it laid the foundation for realization and conceptualization of my own parenting strategies and philosophies and how I would work with future parents, teens, and my own children.

Whose story, told or untold, resonates with you the most?

"Healing from the Horror: A Mother's Love" resonates with me most because it is a personal story about a member of my own family. But, more importantly, it demonstrates how even through the worst of circumstances parents can become winners in their own regard by parenting and healing themselves. This story has a heart-wrenching beginning but a glorious end.

What is the meaning behind the graphic illustration on the back of the book?

The illustration on the back is a precursor of the cover of volume 2 of *Raising a Winner*. The book is actually a two-part series, and this illustration can be viewed in one of two ways. You could view it as a mother and father looking at their former selves in the mirror or a child looking at what they might become. The caricatures themselves are representative of the sorority and fraternity of which my husband and I are members.

In your own words, what does Grow and Go mean to you?

Grow and Go® means to release the parenting reins and allow children to become independent thinkers.

What do you hope readers gather from purchasing your book?

I hope that readers can identify with one or more short stories that will trigger their own ability to allow their children to Grow & Go®.

Will there be a part two?

Yes, this book is comprised of thirty-seven actual interviews, and this first volume represents the foundational stories. The next subset of short stories will dive deeper into parenting aspects with older children once they have graduated from high school and are now experiencing college life and real world aspects of adulthood.

Do you have plans to author any other books in the near future? Will they be fictional, self-help, or other?

Yes, my next release was actually written before *Raising a Winner*, however, due to the fictional aspects of its story line, I felt that this work would be the best to unveil as a first publication.

Lightning Source UK Ltd.
Milton Keynes UK
UKHW02n0324100118
315810UK00006B/21/P